Pronoia

By: Mahogany Soul

Copyright Email: authorstillzweena@gmail.com

ISBN: 978-1-7369936-4-4

DEDICATION

For baby MuZuri and little girls residing in show me states.
You are the love of the light being.
I hope you know

ACKNOWLEDGMENTS

In crafting this ode to pronoia, to the serendipitous winds and the unseen hands guiding us toward light, I have been graced with an abundance of support, love, and cosmic serendipity. This journey, woven from the ethereal threads of an optimistic universe, has been nothing short of magical. To all who have been part of this journey, knowingly or unknowingly, I offer my heartfelt gratitude.

To the universe, for its mysterious ways and whispered secrets that dance on the edges of consciousness, inspiring awe, and a profound sense of connectedness. You are my muse, my canvas, my eternal source of wonder.

To my family, whose unwavering belief in the goodness that lies ahead and behind, in the seen and unseen, has been my foundation. Your love is the embodiment of pronoia, always guiding me back to the light.

To my friends, fellow travelers in this adventure, who see the world not as it is but as it could be. Your optimism, laughter, and shared moments of synchronicity have been the stars guiding me through the darkest nights.

To my mentors and the poets who came before me, who taught me to listen to the whispers of the universe and to trust the process. Your wisdom has been a beacon, illuminating the path with the glow of shared human experience and the power of belief.

To the strangers who crossed my path at just the right moment, offering smiles, kind words, or acts of kindness when least expected but most needed. You are the living proof of the universe's benevolence, the face of pronoia in its most beautiful form.

And to you, the reader, who has found this poem and perhaps a piece of yourself within its lines. May it serve as a reminder that you are never alone, that every moment is a thread in the grand tapestry of existence, woven with intention and love by the universe itself.

This poem is a testament to the beauty of believing that everything happens for us, not to us. To all who have contributed to this belief, in ways big and small, your presence in this journey has been a gift of immeasurable value. Thank you for being a part of this conspiracy of support, love, and boundless optimism.

Contents

Pronoia 5

Root Chakras & Rocket ships 11

Shushya 14

Milk of the Poppy 19

Views 20

Crows by the Murder 22

A Run Away From Home 24

Kintsugi 28

Monday's Business 30

The Reveal 32

The Recovery of Autumn 34

PRONOIA 37

PRONOIA 40

Pronoia

honey heaven inhabited her petals
Before she ever knew it
Twas seasoned, sweet with powder sugar perfection
And she didn't even know it

deliciousness was built into the building blocks of a peace
She only reasoned peacefully
Peacefully easy
In secret
She was the love of the light being
Dark skin prayers
Controlled her tongue
Before she even knew it
Glued it in unfaithful
I love you hallelujahs
on a fiat currency
Backed by nothing
More valuable than a black dream
A black dream
Broke up like
So much black love
Akin to a hope
More fodder for suckas
To suckle on
In supplication
With no real faith

In the invisible wings of black things
Unseen
Intentionally
Intentionally
So, you never
Even
Know
It

You'd never even know it
Life being a constant state of show me
Mu Zuri
You are loved
Though
Based on what's shown
I'm sure you'd
Hardly
Even know it

Black love
Is such a sacred thing
The feared dark magic
Fragmented
Frayed
Forgone
Fighting
Flighty
Flagrant
Full
Out
Festering
A good

fast away from mastery
Feeling
Fleeting
Though it inhabits the very fabric of the thing
We black folk bring into balance
But you would hardly ever know it.
We literally losing our feet
Dulled by too sweet
Like we ain't sun plumped sugar babies
Full up on watermelon juice
Like we ain't the very fruit of the thing
Quote
"If you were born with dark skin you have a chance, of you are born with a white skin and you have money you have a tremendous chance, if you are born poor with white skin you have nothing" end quote
Ain't that something?
Nevell Goddard said that
Said that
just being black means
You are blessed with something
If only somehow
You could know it
Your black skin is akin to a currency
Did you know it?
The sun feeds us like we are the very light beings
While attempting to scorch away the non melinated
Got them so uncomfortable they want to burn away the sun
Did you know it?
This hair
All lambs wool

Like Jesus
Is connected to the ether
Feeding our depleted vitamin D
Did you know it
You could literally change
The trajectory of your day
By getting outside
and getting
some of God's given
sun on your face
Did you
ever
even
know it,
light beings?
Why do you think
Things seem to find a way to make you forget yourself?
Roots and foods are meant to be
Medicine
Instead of just a full belly
Did you know it?
Your frequency is affected by
Words and music you tune into
Did you know it?
The spelling of your child's name is a spell
Spoken each time they are called upon
Did you know it?
If you did
Well,
Id hardly even know it

This is a constant state of show me
Baby Mu Zuri
You are loved
In a way you may need to remember
With a bank full of something
That feels like fools gold
glued to faithful I love you hallelujahs in a fiat currency
Backed by nothing
You can prove
Can you get used to a faith with out proof
Until it comes to fruit
Can you know it?
Already
In the inner way hope
Of your show me soul
Do you know?
The honey heaven that inhabited your petals
Already
Haphazardly
Handed
Hurriedly
Hindering
Hindsight
A highlight
Holding
A Heresy
Of heralding
Hope
With hallowed hands
Praying over you in the distance
In a tongue that so silence
It seasons the breeze in prays

Asè
It is done
If only you'd know it
That girl was gilded in golden
Before she ever knew it

Seasoned her sweet with powder sugar perfection
And she didn't even know it
Fleur-de-lis
Deliciousness built into the building blocks of a peace
She only reasoned peacefully
Peacefully
Easy
In secret
She was the love of the light being
Can you know it
With the Pronoia
That the world aspires to design things to the delight of God and in your favor
And you don't even know it.

Root Chakras & Rocket ships

Own it
Your magic, your madness
This moment
Your soul
that pose
Show me a world
Through your glasses
Covered in rose

Let us experience
This universe you own
Expose those who
Care to know
To the bliss of your full ownership
You got it
Own it
Your lips
Your grace
Your skin
That face
That waist weighted down
From that rice heavy plate
The splendid way you smile
When you're favorite song comes on is a thing of beauty
That could launch a thousand love poems
Own all off them
Every page
Every stage

Every stroke
Every cut
Bleed the ink
Change the state
Of the blank page
For good.
Own
Every right modicum of your magnificently magnanimous magnetism
A living testament
To be a woman mid experience
And open enough to the fullness of her existence to own this bitch
With out question
Without asking for permission
Without letting someone's perspective
Stand between you and your decisions or your conviction
Live in your vision
From your hips
A Griffen
From the root prove
That evolution begins with
Brown eye
I am
From location of letching
And release of excrement
Begin
Again
After the fall arise
It's an inside job
For your savior to arrive
The one who lied with the lie must die
And in her wake

She
wills
your spirit
The deed of
Owning your experience
Own it now
While the blood still pulses
Blue in your closed veins
And pain keeps proving
You got nerve
You deserve
To be owned
And owner
Soul be master body be slave
Every muscle you can muster be primed
Mind be tamed
Sword be sharp shield be God gilded
Own this shit
For it is yours
This moment currently
Your madness
Your magic
my heart
Renew my faith
In the magic of living art
Fuck their table
Take your place amongst the sky full of stars.

Shushya

Every other day
i sit bear feet
Criss criss apple sauce
Surrounded by green
With the weight of the world on my chest
It would seem
I take a minute here and I breathe
In Shushya
I become the trees
The sanctity of being solid in a windstrown world
I become the branches
Unfurling and waving at the flow through of things
I am thankful in this moment
Its like my prayers
Got wangs on em
I am a murder of crows run off with my woes
I become the root,
making fare with the firmament
Through a terra firma firm
Submitting to the subterrestrial
I go deep
because i know
That though
scary things are buried there
Its the only way that i can grow
And i grow
Shushya
upward

Breathing through my belly
Fortifying my gut instinct
A Solid that knotties up my pain body
With purposeful fortitude
My attitude is different
Because by gratitude
is prayerful
It's a work song of the storekeeper
Doing a blessings inventory

An oral
reprogramming of the story
Of the state of the thing
That is my being
Through Shushya
I identify my strength
and I realize
I got whole stores of good things
On me
I mean look at me
I'm breathing
And i be
Like a tree planted by the water
I remind myself
I'm the daughter of Oshun
Every drip
I bring
Is a damn good thing
Even the breaking
of water at my eyes
Supplies me with
A wet release

And i place them between my palms like Ase'

And i say one last
thank you
So even when it seems that I have
no things
I know
all things are
called to be
A moment ago I was Atlas then
All at once I was a tree
You see how many blessings I got on me?
And with all I've got to work with
I work with it
Warm and purple in my thankful praying hands
I work with the universe to transmute
The prayers from the woes
Like lead into gold.
And so you know the recipe
For Shushya
blessings inventory alchemy

Now family
I ask you
Lovingly
Take a moment
And breath
with me
Lets work with the Shushya
in your being

You Breathing?
Your heart beating?
A beautiful thing ain't it?

Them two hands for making light work

Of prayed over deeds
praying hands
And Prostrate knees
Did you pray today?
Body broken bedside
Thankful for where your soul resides
Have you access to clean water and green food
What you feeding you?
What you read this week?
Did you peak yet?
Can you tweak that cut
to get a lil more meat?
Did you smile at someone
You light blooming being
Do you recognize that special sauce you bringing?
Have you flexed?
or thrown around your weight?
What you waiting for baby?
What's it gone take?
What's going to convince you
To
get out of your own way?
You abusing them excuses
When you going to stop playing?
I'm asking you this, for your sake,
Ain't you rested yet?
It's been a long time,
you been sleep on yourself?
Did you dust off some stuff
Put some old stuff away?
Cluttered mind cluttered space
Have you cleaned up your place?
Or fragrance your neck

Look after yourself
like you want some respect?

It's about time you start making
better decisions
Eat a little fruit
Sweeten
your disposition
What's it going to take
For you to acknowledge your wealth
Wake up little giant
Don't sleep on yourself

And the many blessings
In Your praying hands will
overflow
Like salt turned to honey
And
lead weight changed to gold
Shushaya uses the magic you hold
If only
you'll sit under a tree
and be
be still
be thankful and know
and that's on my mahogany soul

Milk of the Poppy

My Beloved Poppy,
I reclaim you
The matters at hand have become to calloused
To receive them without a smarting
The Fingers can no longer be counted on for softness
The raw diet isn't palatable here
Even to the hungriest of mouths
The laughter is ever
Louder than the listening
They told me only of your poison
Like you aint the stuff of strong medicine
So Poppy,
I'll reclaim you
And learn to take you in slow optimist doses.
And wait
For the type of fragility it takes
To be a healing blade

Views

It's out
The everything
Unapologetically
Existing
Under the light of the age of Aquarius
Knowing
Being unarguably
Resolute
Its uncovered
Like the aftermath of hurricanes on
The peace
of graveyards
Just
Raising up the dead
That wades in the wake of
The Previously drowned
Conclusions i laid to rest
Leaving me to piece together
The uncovered bones
Escsvating my faith
Laced with Guilt for questioning
What a Godly heart should make
Of things that refuse to live
I know Gangrene requires a clean cut to save the blood
But
I'm also aware
Of the gravity of Sampson hair
And yet i must identify what must be cut off

And which benefits from mending
Dead ends and
Fences are tricky things that way
I mean you cant mend a single post
Without questioning if the integrity of what's left will hold
But Knowing

is abundantly conclusive
Abundantly
And absolute
Just feast your eyes on all this proof.
It's out now
The everything
Understanding the unchecked nature
Of wayward love
On the freedom of the
Changling
No longer remaining
In the dual mind ambiguity of confusion
I dangle here no more
Even the bees taste the sweetness
From the gossiping breeze alone
Everyone knows
Of its existence now
Its all out on the line
Thats the beauty of light
It proves
What can be seen
Does change my views

Crows by the Murder

Where have the little birdies gone
How ever are they safe?
When every other natural thing
Gets washed away with rain
The trunks of trees find ease of root
As puddles slowly pool
And little boys lost little toys
Relent to current's rule
A sewer grate stands guard at gate
Catching everything come loosed
A washing off of brick and cloth
of metal tin and roof
A church of clapping hands tap windows panes
Rinsing subtle grains of sin
As everything the sky can see
Gets baptized in the wind
I close my eyes and sight relents to orchestra of storm
A rock and roll of thunder claps
that barrels through the calm
Through dancing lighting and 'sippi counts
My consternation hums
As gentle heart beat readies for
the coming of the drums
Little creatures long since have scurried
Burrowed in their nook

And I voyeur from my shelter in the bottom of a book
There is magic mixed with meant to be in all the darkness may belie
Still I wonder where do birdies go when the storm takes back the sky

A Run Away From Home

On this morning
I woke up in a body with heavy bruised hands
And calloused over features
A thin crust away from softness
A body bloated
Bruised and battered
A body contaminated
Put asunder
Innundated by persistent skin people thinking
Before the sun
Come through my window.
This body heavy in all the ways that spite my lightness.
This body biiiiiig.
And too heavy
To handle before the sun even cracked my morning open.
But
On this particular dawn
The drawn blinds Shaded the light to the delight of my delicate eyes while only the bravest slither of amber anxious at its edge set the brighter precedence of this day.
And I, in this body I woke up in, all weighted down in matter of fact and matter
a fact that felt like a pin down to the bed at my shoulders. Succumb to the lead of a luxury I'm told I can't afford.

Rest

And I in this body lay resting
To the joy of my soul
And the bend of my will
Lay resting
Until
I lifted myself
And left the body on the bed
I lifted myself light
And left the body on the bed
I stretched to an expansion bigger
Than the body on the bed
I spread till my abstract hips kissed
The brave amber slither at my window
And i hovering lightly above
the body on the bed
spread all over the world
I Unfurled
command my wounds
Now
They are no longer aggravating dark space
In the paintings
pinking up in pleasure and permanent ink
I am storied
are archipelagos
Who's waters
Love must prepare to cross
Testing the meddle of your swim good
Now
my body is Pangea
At peace with the drifting
Gifting pieces of my breaking as seeds
For wondering clansman to proudly plant
along their travels

Trespassers renamed me pandora making assumptions about my purpose
And planting fear in the light where the dark can't come.
I spread so
You'd hardly even know I'm Eden
I get to be the peace in the meant to bes'

I touched the goodness of the whole of the world with my hands left behind
With my body
On the bed.
And
On this morning
When
I opened my eyes again
Seated in this body again, I hold fast to the memory of being as big as the whole world
from the love side
I open my eyes and try to feel that big
Again
Connected to these hands.
And I in this body again
Try to remember
That I can
I can
make magic
make mahem
Marry the madness
I make love
i make a mess
I make a mission
I can make light
And a life

Of learning from the blood signs of
The little cuts left
on this body

I can make a mastery
Of remembering that beyond this body
I am extending a bigger to the edge of the world
And I
In this body
Recall how big I could be if

I get up from this bed
And spread
So I take myself in a little bit of light at a time
Holding hands with the amber edge urging me
anxiously from my window
At a time when time itself feels like a weighting on this
body

Again

Kintsugi

The artist chooses the finest porcelain from the desk
And
Examines it from varied perspectives
A detective in his inspection of the perfection that is his selection
This specimen
So delicate
Snow flake like
Intricately
Innocently
Instinctively
A one of a kind masterpiece
He thinks
He breaths in awe of his luck
Well that was
Until the hammer struck
But the artist views the
chaos of the pieces
As a master does mystery
as one with apophenia
picturing the beauty in broken things
The beginning
Of an ending
He sows my broken heart
Close the holes
He guilds my greatness
together with gold
He mends my soul with an artist's hand
And the tenderness that only an artists can

Said
"I see your broken and I name you healed"
So
Though it all seems doomed from the start
And at times it feels that I'm falling apart
I've come so far
From where i started
Snd though this part may feel the hardest
I'm a work in progress
Of a thoughtful artist
I'm the working clay
If a work of art
From the top of my head
To bottom of my beautifully broken heart

Monday's Business

I'm trying to train my Sundays to stay out of my Last
Mondays business.
Time traveling to the past
Always seems to zap my energy
Requiring deep rest
I am not depressed I am tired
Of trying to sweep floors that don't exist no more
The past is unchangeable
But more is possible
From right here
Criss cross applesauce
Surrounded by fear
I walk through the valley
Till the light we all pull towards calls me
and re-absorbs me
I am the light
Delighted by the fruit heavy benefit of my light touch
Eyes closed
Awake for the first time
Mind trained on the ways of transcendent behavior
Forward is inevitable
Motion intentional
Weapon is this woman vessel
I'm gone step so heavy
That the crevices formed by my full weight
Will make way for gardens
Abundant things
A place of peace
A retreat to evenings in my tiny piece of Eden

Where I am the oil
Fossil fuel
Enriched by my dense bones
Oh I'm gone one this space
But I can only own it one moment at a time
So I'm training my mind
To make smarter decisions
First order is to stay out of last Monday's business.

The Reveal

As you speak
I string your promise together like
polo ponies

They too
Are playing their very best game
And
Since I'm in attendance I attempt to participate
I match my hand claps with the crowds
Aping their whoops, hollers and swoons
I am the great pretender, I acutely match their moves
You'd hardly even notice that I don't know what I'm
doing
And Yet
the rumble of their thunder steps
Shake my heart right in my chest
And the swings in my direction
Always seem to take my breath
They kick up hearty plugs of dirt
I remind myself,

I mean...
somebody's in trouble
You left behind so many holes
At least the horse's excrement will have a place to go.

You ask me if I'm listening and I say
"Yes, I see you"
As I watch your game of words
And
I try not to get confused
Or maybe I'm just childish
Thinking everything's a game
But the space between congruencies
Seems a perfect place for play
And the thing about a guarded girl
Is she knows to well to be real
That words could never say as much as patterns will
reveal.

The Recovery of Autumn

Rouge on lips cover the smoke stains
Henna to hide the greys
She's been looking for a cover
Thats why she covers herself this way
Wig hide undisciplined roots
To Cover

cover skin
Covered in chaos

The clever
learn to cloak
To find cover in 3/4ths of cloth
Cover the sweet of your leaves
Else you'll be covered in salivating
Symbionts seeking cover
From a life
Covered in failing women
Covered in failing men
To cover our esteem from the scene of so many falling leaves
But.

Ground cover does produce
A Blanket Cover of warmth
For fertile earth
Covered in wind tousled seeds
By spring this place will be covered in green again.
Mother earths unwavering proof of recovery.

The following poems are contributions by other authors who enjoyed and were inspired by the idea of PRONOIA. Please send your contributuions to @onmymahoganysoul @ gmail.com to join the movement. Special thanks go out to

PRONOIA

Black love is such a sacred thing
The feared dark magic

If I seriously had to go through it to get to it?
Choosing struggle and again, getting through it
And again
And again

Pronoia once the exclusive elixir of the entitled mass
At last, proven to be more than hippie horoscope spin
The universe conspires to my good- I wink

With a language orphaned of words to describe emotion
We speak of love metaphorically
Such power defies all attempts to conceal it

If I did not see it feel it

I would not believe it know it

happy endings were not presumptions,

but suspicions gone rogue.

My imagination ran past Disneyland

and took a walk in the park with you

3 years later, its all "I do" and "I do too"

This I know.

Better with than without

We merge just before we touch

On nucleic levels

the sun feeds us as though we are light beings

and one walk in the park sun soaked tokin and no stroking

Rendered precious by giant hands engulfing mine, 2fer

Inner child peeking from the eyes of Fully Grown her

Is it arrogant that she knew?

Dark skin prayers controlled her tongue before she even knew it

The Goddess on a leash, set free with a kiss

I am all that I am and then some

and goddamn if I didn't know what I knew

with words thick with Bahamian nuance

Backed by nothing

More valuable than a black dream

Love spoken like a hushed prayer-

I Do.

PRONOIA

Black love is such a sacred thing
The feared dark magic
Is it arrogance if I knew it?
If I seriously had to go through it to get to it?
Choosing struggle and again, getting through it
And again

Pronoia once the exclusive elixir of the entitled mass
At last, Proven to be more than hippie horoscope spin
The universe conspires to my good- I win.

With a language orphaned of words to describe emotion
We speak of love metaphorically
Such power defies all attempts to conceal it

If I did not see it feel it
I would not believe it know it
happy endings were not presumptions,
but suspicions gone rogue.
My imagination ran past Disneyland
and took a walk in the park with you
3 years later, its all "I do" and "I do too"

This I know.
Better with than without
We merge just before we touch
On nucleic levels
the sun feeds us as though we are light beings

and one walk in the park sun soaked tokin and no stroking
Rendered precious by giant hands engulfing mine, 2fer
Inner child peeking from the eyes of Fully Grown her
Is it arrogant that she knew?

Dark skin prayers controlled her tongue before she even knew it
The Goddess on a leash, set free with a kiss
I am all that I am and then some
and goddamn if I didn't know what I knew
with words thick with Bahamian nuance
Backed by nothing
More valuable than a black dream
Love spoken like a hushed prayer-
I Do.
Her silence, Confronts the origin of her sound Before it leaps abound... Sometimes, "A good fast away from mastery" is required When her 'high ways' are too congested with everyone else desires So she switches lanes to receive the message And own the direction of her own drive..... There are moments that humble her noise into submission Where the cadence of simply breathing Gifts the sweetest listen..... Inhales and exhales write her a love letter And may love let her scent kiss it With the true essence of living Never knowing the day nor hour When things may be different Yet, She grants herself the permission To be in her light being.... No overextensions... No explanation for her "no's".... No guilt trips Or Compromising her rising No shrinking... Just being.... Marinating in her own speech So the juice matures her palate And splashes against her roof Savoring some for

herself inside of her own cheeks Before she speaks Knowing it's ok to let them drink her silence Even with "life being a constant state of "show me" She's showing The cities that are sitting inside her That sometimes, Silence confronts the origins of sounds Resting deep beneath its soil That require the patience To cultivate and emerge within its own wealth Before it expands into hands That try to mold it into their own image With no compassion or even the attempt to understand Its vision or plans....-Kimbrella Renea

ABOUT THE AUTHOR

Mahogany Soul (Edwina Simmons) is an emerging member of the poetry community as co host Self Care Sunday for Poets with, FlySpeak Open Mic with Mojavi Sundiata Emi and Shut up and Spit on Epiphany Radio Network, a ForReal Entertainment network. Edwina is also a performing member with the HoneyDripper Poetry Collective and the When Women Speak Collective. She has performed in The Lincoln Park Music Festival's 50th Anniversary of Hip Hop, Dripfest, Artistry Live Decatur, Women Wine and Words, Poetry in the Bricks, Newark's Down the Ro' Series and many more.

Find her on instagram @mymahoganysoul on her website at edwinatheauthor where signed books, performances, and bookings can be found.

www.ingramcontent.com/pod-product-compliance
Lightning Source LLC
LaVergne TN
LVHW051022080826
845145LV00009B/2749

* 9 7 8 1 7 3 6 9 9 3 6 4 4 *